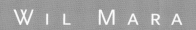

HAZMAT REMOVAL
WORKER

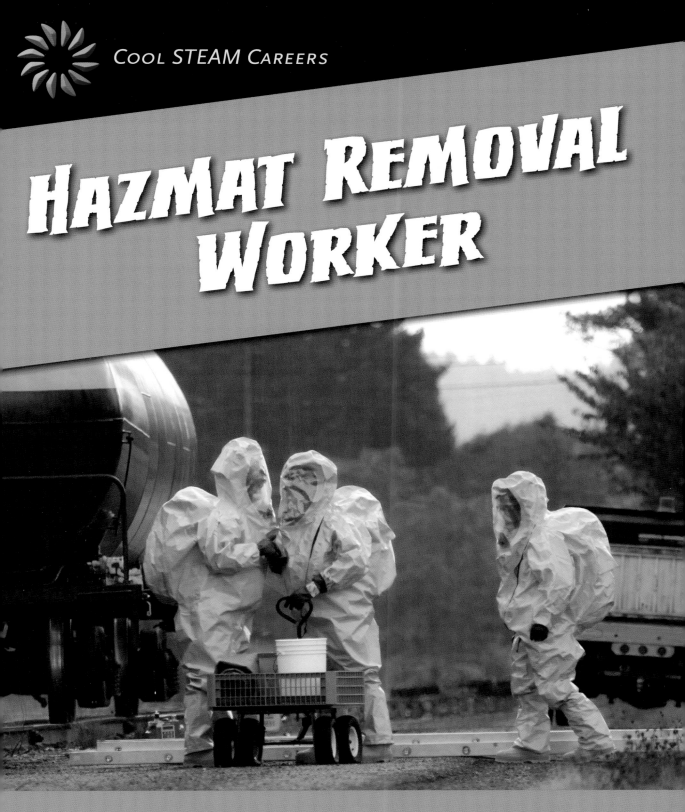

WIL MARA

Published in the United States of America by Cherry Lake Publishing
Ann Arbor, Michigan
www.cherrylakepublishing.com

Content Adviser: Dr. Karen L. Knee, Assistant Professor of Environmental Science, American University, Washington, DC.
Reading Adviser: Marla Conn, ReadAbility, Inc.

Photo Credits: ©BenDC/Thinkstock, cover, 1, 16; ©Africa Studio/Shutterstock Images, 5; ©ggw1962/Shutterstock Images, 6; ©IkeHayden/Shutterstock Images, 9; ©davetroesh/depositphotos, 11, 15; ©njari/CanStockPhoto, 12; ©Sergey Kamshylin/Shutterstock Images, 17; ©Overcrew55/Dreamstime.com, 18; ©Tigergallery/Shutterstock Images, 21; ©Krzysztof Slusarczyk/Shutterstock Images, 22; ©Endostock/Dreamstime.com, 25; ©Wellphotos/Dreamstime.com, 26; ©Kodda/Shutterstock Images, 29

Library of Congress Cataloging-in-Publication Data

Mara, Wil, author.
Hazmat removal worker / Wil Mara.
        pages cm. — (Cool STEAM careers)
 Summary: "Readers will learn what it takes to succeed as a hazmat removal
worker. The book also explains the necessary educational steps, useful
character traits, and daily job tasks related to this career, in the
framework of the STEAM (Science, Technology, Engineering, Art, and Math)
movement. Photos, a glossary, and additional resources are included."— Provided by publisher.
 Audience: Ages 8-12.
 Audience: Grades 4 to 6.
 Includes bibliographical references and index.
 ISBN 978-1-63362-004-9 (hardcover) — ISBN 978-1-63362-043-8 (pbk.) — ISBN 978-1-63362-082-7 (pdf) —
ISBN) 978-1-63362-121-3 (ebook) 1. Hazardous substances—Juvenile literature. 2. Hazardous waste site remediation—
Juvenile literature. 3. Hazardous waste management industry—Vocational guidance—Juvenile literature. I. Title.

T55.3.H3M245 2015
363.17023—dc23   2014031692

Cherry Lake Publishing would like to acknowledge the work of
The Partnership for 21st Century Skills. Please visit www.p21.org
for more information.

Printed in the United States of America
Corporate Graphics

ABOUT THE AUTHOR

Wil Mara is an award-winning and best-selling author of more than 150 books, many of which are educational titles for young readers. Further information about his work can be found at www.wilmara.com.

TABLE OF CONTENTS

STEAM is the acronym for Science, Technology, Engineering, Arts, and Mathematics. In this book, you will read about how each of these study areas is connected to a career in hazmat removal.

A Concern for Public Safety

Becky was thirsty after a bike ride. Just as she was about to fill a glass with cold tap water, her mom ran into the kitchen. She said, "Don't drink the water!"

"Why not?" asked Becky. "I always have water after a bike ride."

"I just heard a news bulletin warning people not to use the water in our area," her mom explained. "There was a chemical spill that made its way into our water supply. We're not supposed to drink the water or use it for bathing or brushing teeth or to wash dishes."

Tap water is usually safe to drink—but not always.

A scientist tests drinking water in a lab to be sure it is safe to use.

"That sounds dangerous!" Becky exclaimed. "What else did you learn from the news?"

"The governor has called in specialists to test the water and hazardous material workers to begin the cleanup," Mom replied.

"Thank goodness we heard the news before using the water," Becky said.

Hazardous materials are those that are dangerous because they are toxic or explosive. They exist inside and outside the home and can cause problems where you might not expect them.

Hazardous materials became much more common during **industrialization**, which began to boom in the United States around 1860. At the same time people began to understand their dangers. Factories were built at a record pace and workers began using and in some cases creating new, unknown materials. Around the house, hazardous materials include bleach, ammonia, gasoline, and drain-cleaning fluid.

THINK ABOUT ART

*In the field of hazardous **waste** removal, you may have to exercise innovative thinking. The real challenge, then, is to pull together all of your education, experience, instinct, and creative energy to come up with solutions that might never have been considered before.*

Hazardous materials occur in nature as well. They've been there for millions of years. **Mercury**, for example, occurs under normal conditions as a silvery liquid. It is used to make thermometers and other scientific instruments. But it is a very dangerous substance. So is uranium, which is highly **radioactive**. It's used for everything from decorative glassblowing to the production of military-grade weapons.

Today, hazardous material workers—or hazmat workers, for short—deal with everything from oil-based paints and **asbestos** to **nuclear waste**. Hazmat workers might be called to factories or disaster sites. The hours can be long and the work difficult, but it is also personally very rewarding. The technology for handling, **neutralizing**, and, in some cases, disposing of hazardous materials is better than ever. But many serious challenges remain.

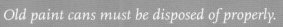

WHAT IT TAKES

Being in excellent health is important for a hazmat removal worker. You may have to wear a heavy protective suit for long hours. The suit's added weight and design make it hard for you to move. A hazmat removal worker should have excellent decision-making skills, especially when under pressure to reduce risks. Paying attention to details and checking and rechecking your work are necessary in this job. The smallest amount of a hazardous substance can cause big problems. Having mechanical skills, or a willingness to learn mechanical

Following safety rules is critical for hazmat workers.

skills, is also helpful, since you'll be using powerful equipment fairly often.

A basic education is required for entry-level hazmat positions. Some people get into the field with only a high school diploma. But, as with almost any other profession, the more education you have, the better your chances of being hired. Some schools offer associate's degrees, or 2-year college degrees, that relate to hazardous waste. There are professionals with bachelor's, masters, and Ph.D. degrees who work in the hazmat field doing a variety of jobs.

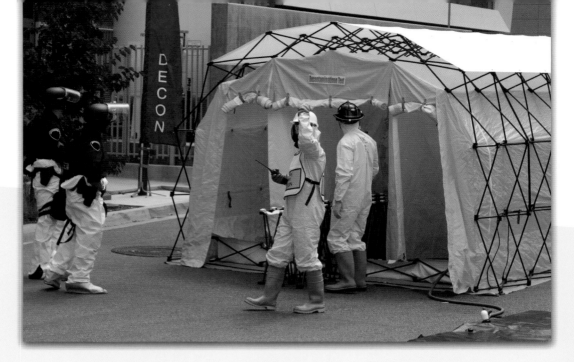

Hazmat workers receive training while on the job.

In the classroom, future hazmat workers will learn about everything from smart safety practices to the numerous dangerous materials that will be encountered and the correct use of equipment to handle them. A **simulation** could be part of your training. In a classroom setting, you might learn about specific hazardous materials, such as asbestos, **mold**, or nuclear waste.

Beyond the classroom, you can expect on-site training, which will put you into a real environment with a qualified instructor. You'll be required to have a minimum number of on-site hours of experience before you can attain certification or licensing. Forty hours is common in many states. Your training may also need to meet the standards of certain agencies, such as the Occupational Safety and Health Administration. This is a federal government agency concerned with assuring a safe working environment.

The cost of such training varies tremendously. Oftentimes companies pay for the training and education of their employees.

THINK ABOUT MATH

Your math skills need to be sharp, as you'll be working with dangerous chemicals from time to time and might need to mix them, which would require precise measurements. Making a mistake could make the situation worse. People's lives may depend on your success in double-checking your work.

CHAPTER 3

ON THE JOB

Most hazmat removal workers are required to travel to different locations on a regular basis. Usually they stay within their "home range," but occasionally they go to places that require air travel. Sometimes they work inside, sometimes outside. And once a problem is solved, it's time to move on to the next one. In disaster situations, a hazmat removal worker may have to travel to the location and stay there for a long time, sometimes weeks or even months.

Effective hazmat removal requires cooperation

Special breathing equipment is often necessary in a hazmat situation.

among the workers. It is very much like going into battle, where the hazardous material is the enemy and you and your co-workers are the soldiers. As with any other military unit, your chances of success are greatly increased if you work well together.

One of the most important aspects of hazmat removal is called **containment**. This means first identifying the hazardous material, then taking steps to keep it in a confined place. For a chemical spill, a hazmat worker needs to determine the extent of the spill, then make

A fuel spill from a tanker train is hazardous material and must be dealt with carefully.

sure it doesn't spread any farther. This might require marking an area as off-limits to other people.

A common next step is to remove the hazardous material. This means transferring it from the affected area and into a proper **receptacle**. This is where safety and proper knowledge of all equipment are crucial, because this is where you will come into closest contact with the material. You must wear all the proper gear and follow all the safety practices because mistakes could be fatal. Once the materials are safely secured in the proper receptacles,

To Caleb, Joshua, and Noah
—P.Y.S.

For Doug
—R.C.

AUTHOR'S NOTE

I was four years old when most of this story takes place. It is based on my memories, as well as my sisters' and my father's, and on stories I have been told by others who were there. While I have tried to be as accurate as possible, I do not recall conversations word for word. Still, I do clearly remember their spirit, and have tried to capture it in these pages, along with a sense of the civil rights movement, as seen through the eyes of a young child.

ACKNOWLEDGMENTS

I am eternally grateful to my sisters, Andrea and Lisa, for sharing their stories with me; to Daddy, for raising me right and loving me always; to Jeffrey Goldberg, for giving me my big break; to Richard Abate, for taking a chance on me, and to Tina Wexler, for carrying the ball; to Anne Schwartz, for holding my hand and expertly guiding me through this whole process; to Raul Colón, for bringing this story to life so beautifully; and to my husband, Hilary, for his unparalleled love, support, and encouragement.

Text copyright © 2010 by Paula Young Shelton
Illustrations copyright © 2010 by Raul Colón

All rights reserved.
Published in the United States by
Schwartz & Wade Books,
an imprint of Random House Children's Books,
a division of Random House, Inc., New York.

Schwartz & Wade Books and the colophon
are trademarks of Random House, Inc.

Visit us on the Web!
www.randomhouse.com/kids

Educators and librarians, for a variety of teaching tools,
visit us at www.randomhouse.com/teachers

Library of Congress Cataloging-in-Publication Data
Shelton, Paula Young.
Child of the civil rights movement / Paula Young Shelton ;
illustrated by Raul Colón. — 1st ed.
  p. cm.
ISBN 978-0-375-84314-3 (trade)
ISBN 978-0-375-95414-6 (glb)
1. Shelton, Paula Young—Juvenile literature. 2. Selma to
Montgomery Rights March (1965 : Selma, Ala.)—Juvenile
literature. 3. Civil rights movements—Alabama—Selma—
History—20th century—Juvenile literature. 4. African
Americans—Civil rights—Alabama—Selma—History—
20th century—Juvenile literature. 5. Selma (Ala.)—
Race relations—History—20th century—Juvenile literature.
I. Colón, Raul. II. Title.
F334.S4S54 2010
323.1196'073076147—dc22
2008045855

The text of this book is set in Aged.
The illustrations were created by laying a wash on watercolor paper using Winsor & Newton Aureolin Yellow.
The final images were drawn in lead pencil, followed by numerous washes in sepias and browns.
Layers of colored pencil were added, and the images were finished with black lithograph pencil.

MANUFACTURED IN MALAYSIA

1 3 5 7 9 10 8 6 4 2

First Edition